Applied Metapsychology Dictionary

Compiled by Frank A. Gerbode, MD

AMI Press

Applied Metapsychology Dictionary
Compiled by Frank A. Gerbode, MD

First Printing: September 2019

ISBN 978-1-61599-474-8 paperback
ISBN 978-1-61599-475-5 hardcover
ISBN 978-1-61599-476-2 eBook

AMI Press is an imprint of
Applied Metapsychology International
5145 Pontiac Trail
Ann Arbor, MI 48105

Email info@tir.org
web www.tir.org

Contents

Introduction iii

Glossary 1

Commonly Used Abbreviations in Applied Metapsychology.....53

About Applied Metapsychology International 55

Introduction

The term "metapsychology" (small m) means, briefly: The science that unifies mental and physical experience. Its purpose is to discover the rules that apply to both. It is a study of the person, their abilities and experience, as seen from their own point of view. Applied Metapsychology (AMP) is the subject that puts the principles of metapsychology to work for the purpose of relieving traumatic stress, promoting personal growth and development, and empowering people to improve the quality of their lives.

This dictionary includes most of the terms used in Applied Metapsychology. Working out a proper and consistent vocabulary for metapsychology has been a continual compromise between what sounds graceful in ordinary English and what conveys a precise meaning. Many of our terms also occur in normal speech in a sense similar to, but usually not exactly the same as, that given here, just as physics uses terms like "mass", "density", and "energy" in a specialized and more precise way. Natural language is preferred instead of inventing new terms, because their meaning is similar enough to normal usage to give the reader an intuitive idea of what is meant, while the metapsychological definition provides the needed precision for the subject. However, a few terms have required a stretch in meaning, as it is clumsy at times to use a phrase when a single unusual or stretched word would be easier to fit into sentences. Two words are especially stretched in this dictionary and in our materials, because they are commonly used in both a specialized and non-specialized sense. These are *"having"* in its various forms and *"thing"* (formerly "entity"). These are put in italics when they are being used in the specialized AMP sense.

The terminology has evolved over time. This dictionary gives the current lexicon, but some changes will likely occur in the future, and no doubt this dictionary will have to be modified and expanded.

Words defined are given in boldface. In the PDF and the electronic version of this dictionary, an italicized word or phrase within a definition denotes a hyperlink to the definition of that word or phrase elsewhere in the dictionary. In the printed version, only "*having*" and "*thing*" are italicized.

See the appendix of this dictionary for some commonly used abbreviations and acronyms in the subject of Applied Metapsychology

Glossary

Aberration: Distortion of thought, *perception, intention, identity,* and *behavior,* caused by the *traumatic incident network.*

Ability: A combination of *control* and *understanding.* Control is what corresponds, on the *person* side of the *person-world polarity,* to order on the world side. Understanding corresponds to *heuristics.* *"An ability"* is the potential for performing a specific action or type of action, whereas "ability" (used without an article) means a more *general* capability or potentiality. Thus *"an* ability" could be regarded as the exercise of ability in a specific area.

Ability Enhancement: The activity of employing *AMP* techniques after *Life Stress Reduction* to enhance a *viewer*'s abilities.

Ability Enhancement Workshop: One of several workshops that teach the techniques of the different sections of the *Ability Enhancement Viewing Curriculum.*

Ability Enhancement Viewing Curriculum: See *Curriculum.*

Acceptance: A form of *assent* that completes an *activity cycle.* Compare *commitment.*

Access: The ability to receive something causatively. Also (as a verb) to exercise causation in a *receptive* mode. Compare *influence.*

Acknowledgment: An *indication* given by the receiver of a *communication* to the originator of the communication that is intended to convey the *datum* that the communication was received and *comprehended.* It is also an indication, given by the issuer of a request to the *person* who complies, that the issuer is aware of the compliance.

Acting Out: *Behavior* that is caused by the *reactivation* of one or more *traumatic incidents*. It is an unconscious re-enactment of the behavior that occurred at the time of the traumatic incident or incidents as (usually rationalized) behavior directed toward present-time *objects* or people. It may also be behavior influenced by the traumatic incident that has been *reactivated*. The behavior may be appropriate to the past incident or incidents, but it is usually not appropriate to the present situation. Therefore it often has destructive consequences.

Action: An instance of causation by a *person*. The exercise of an *ability*.

Action Plan: In *consultation*_mode, a series of actual steps to be taken in life by the client. The plan is devised by the client with the practitioner acting as *consultant*.

Active: An active *sequence* or *traumatic incident* is one of which a *person* is recently or easily reminded. Compare *inactive*.

Activity: The *action* or actions (*creative* or *receptive*) that a *person* takes in order to fulfill an *intention*.

Activity Cycle (Cycle): The entire history of an activity, from beginning to end. A cycle has a point of *creation* or starting, a period during which it is persisting, continuing, and changing; and a point of ending. For any given *person*, different periods of time are defined by the cycles that exist for that person. Some cycles are brought into being by the *intentions* that rule the various *creative actions*, others by intentions associated with the various *receptive actions*. Formulating an intention gives a person something to do, an activity in which to engage. The activity, the cycle, and the period of time so created last as long as the intention lasts and no longer.

Addictions Program: An *AMP program* for addressing addictions.

Adverse Childhood Experience Studies (ACEs): The studies by Felitti and Anda commencing in 1994 that amply demonstrate the need for the effectiveness of *TIR* and *TIR for children*.

Aesthetics: The appreciation of beauty. A "positive" kind of pleasure, not pleasure derived from *relief* of *pain* or discomfort.

Affection: Affinity directed toward a *person*, not a *thing*. The wish to be close to another person, to share a common space and viewpoint. An impulse toward *communion*. A high degree of affection is referred to as "love". Compare *desire*, *disaffection*.

Affinity: A willingness to be close to, or to assume the viewpoint of, something or someone, to reach for or share space with that *person* or *thing*. It is a willingness to *have* something, or to be close to someone. When directed toward a person, affinity is *affection*; when directed towards a *thing*, it is *desire*. Compare *aversion*.

After the Fact Item: In *TIR*, an *item* that places the *viewer* in a part of an *incident* or incidents that occur after the main trauma. "A feeling of repression", for instance, is probably an after-the-fact item. "Depression about relationships" might be an after-the-fact item as well. A *descriptive item* can equally well be after-the-fact. If the viewer provides the item "The time I was in the hospital with a wounded leg", they may be placing themself in the part of the incident that comes after the real trauma. "The time my leg got wounded" would be safer.

Agenda: See *Session Agenda*.

Alienation: A low degree of *communication, comprehension*, and *affection* which, together, form a descending triad: less communication leads to less comprehension and less affection, less comprehension leads to less affection and less communication, and less affection leads to less communication and less comprehension. The easiest way out of this descending triad is by communicating. The opposite of *communion*.

Alignment: The tendency of different parts of a *person*'s world to fit together properly or to work together harmoniously to further the *intentions* of the person. The opposite of *incongruity*.

Ambivalence: A level of the *Emotional Scale* between Antagonism and Complacency. When one is ambivalent, one is on the borderline between liking or disliking a certain *identity*, *activity*, or experience. This is the emotional level at which one has "mixed feelings". The likelihood of succeeding in the activity is viewed as about equal to the likelihood of failing. The *condition* in the world that corresponds to Ambivalence is *Drudgery*.

Anesthetic Idea: An idea introduced and adhered to in an attempt to avoid *confronting* something painful. Anesthetic ideas tend to be *delusions* or *fixed ideas*.

Applied Metapsychology (AMP): The methods and techniques for applying the principles of *metapsychology* to improving the human condition.

Applied Metapsychology International (AMI): The organization that owns the copyrighted materials of the subject. AMI maintains a central communication point for people using the subject to stay in touch throughout the world, oversees the quality of training worldwide, and maintains the certification program for *facilitators* and *trainers*.

Assent: The action of agreeing, of saying "Yes!" to a *concept*. It is one possible outcome of *considering*, the other possibilities being *dissent* and assignment of a probability. Assent can take two forms: *acceptance*_and *commitment*.

Assertion: A statement or *declaration* that affirms the existence of a particular element of reality and invites agreement. Assertions include *interpretations* and *judgments*. A *facilitator* does not make assertions about the *viewer*'s world or their *case*, except by way of agreeing with something the viewer already *knows* consciously (an *indication*).

Assessing: The action of finding areas of the *viewer's* life (*items*) to which one or more *viewing techniques* can fruitfully be applied, i.e., areas that lie just below the *awareness threshold*. It is always done with a viewer during a *viewing session*.

Assessment list: A *method* of addressing unwanted conditions or *charge*. It is designed to enable a *viewer* to identify specific *items* or issues that are currently *triggered* and of *interest* and to *deactivate* them. The method consists of starting with a predetermined list of questions reflecting different possible areas of charge, addressed to a particular subject or to life in general. The questions are asked, one after another, until the viewer feels interested in, or feels their attention drawn to, one of the questions. The viewer then answers this question to their own satisfaction.

If there is still interest and attention on the question, the *facilitator* follows up using *retrospection* by asking if there is an earlier similar __(whatever it is)__. If so, the viewer talks about that. The "earlier similar" question is asked as many times as needed until that question is handled to the viewer's satisfaction, usually to a *flat point* or small *end point*. On some assessment lists, questions on the list may specify a particular way of dealing with that question, in which case you would follow the prescribed handling instead of using retrospection. Having completed work on one question, the facilitator continues down the list until the viewer finds another question that arouses their interest, etc., until the viewer has an *end point* on the subject of the list or feels there is no more available charge on it.

Assumption (An **Assumption**): A *fact* that refers to, indicates, or implies a *conclusion*. A fact that has meaning. A premise.

Assumption (**of Identity**): Particularization and extension of *identity* through the incorporation of previously external elements (such as *skills*, tools, and *concepts*) as part of the self. The opposite of *shedding*.

Attention: The *intention* to receive. Compare *volition*.

Authority: A *person* or group that is regarded as a source of *knowledge* or *order*. Note that an authority is only an authority for a particular person or group of persons. For someone else, that person or group might not be an authority.

Automatic Attention (**AA**): A mental mechanism by which a *person*'s *mind* processes information prior to presenting it to them as conscious material. It filters *data* based on relevance and on similarity to past events and presents what it regards as appropriate to the person. Thus it sometimes "knows" things that the person themself does not yet consciously *know*, and it is possible to call upon the AA to find *items* that lie just below the *awareness threshold*.

Automaticity: An *action* done by a *person* without their being *aware*, at the time, of doing it. They may be aware that the action is happening but, if so, they do not experience themselves, at the time, as the originator of that action. It seems to be "just happening".

Automatism: An *aberrated*, conditioned, *automaticity*, e.g., a bad habit. Compare *skill*.

Aversion: A refusal or unwillingness to share a space or viewpoint with something or someone, an intention to withdraw from that *person* or *thing*. It is the lower or "negative" portion of the scale of *affinity*. It goes beyond a mere lack of inclination or *willingness* to a positive refusal.

Awareness: *Receptive power*. The ability to engage in *receptive actions*.

Awareness Threshold: The dividing line that separates those *things* of which a *person* can be readily aware from *things* that are repressed. A person can only become aware of the latter by using a special approach, such as a *viewing technique*.

Basic Aversions: Basic types of circumstances people have in their world that they do not like and would like to change. These include *physical aversions* and *situational aversions*.

Basic Goal: A major, long-term *intention* that may be in force during a lifetime or series of lifetimes and which rules the *person*'s basic identity

Basic Identity: An *identity* that occupies the highest point in the *hierarchy of identities* that a *person* can assume, an identity from which a person cannot "step back", or that a person cannot *shed*. It is a matter of speculation what sort of identity this might be. A basic identity is assumed because of, and ruled by, a senior *intention*—a basic *goal* or *purpose*.

Basic TIR (BTIR): A form of *TIR* used to address individual specific known past *traumatic incidents*.

Behavior: Motion of a *person*'s *body*, following his *intentions*.

Being: A *person* or spiritual entity, considered to be separate from a *body* and a *mind*. *viewers* may think of themselves as beings. Some viewers experience the presence of disembodied beings—external to them but, in some sense close by—that seem to exert an influence on them.

Blankness: An experience encountered when there is a failure of *comprehension*. A feeling of emptiness or ignorance that results from the absence of a *concept* that should be there.

Body: The physical organism through which a *person* interacts with the physical world.

Body (of a session): That part of a *session* that comes after *disturbance handling*. It contains the *major action*s of that session.

Built-in Aversion: *Aversion* to uncomfortable bodily sensations (such as feeling too hot, too cold, or nauseated) that under normal circumstances cannot be readily confronted without having a relatively strong intention to do so. These aversions appear to be genetically "built in" to our bodily identity, and most are clearly conducive to survival of the organism.

Button: A stimulus that evokes an involuntary *reaction* such as laughter, a smile, or a flinch.

Case: The sum total of the *charge* a *person* has, together with the *aberration* that results from it.

Case Plan: A written sequence of *viewing techniques*. It is based on data derived from *interviews* and past *sessions* and is designed to enable the *viewer* to accomplish the goals they have expressed for *viewing*. A case plan may include *programs* and *collections*.

Case Planning: The action of deciding which *techniques* should be used with a *viewer* and the order in which they should be done. Case planning is done before starting a *session*, not during a session.

Case Progress: An improvement in the *viewer's* condition; a reduction of *charged* material; an improvement in personal *ability* or in *communion* with others.

CEs: See *Communication Exercises.*

Challenge: A situation that presents difficulties to a *person* that they consider are likely to be surmountable. Compare *stress, traumatic incident.*

Charge: *Repressed,* unfulfilled *intention* resulting in undesirable conditions, such as *stress;* uncomfortable or painful feelings; dulled *awareness,* compulsions, etc. The term is used at times to refer to either that which generates the painful feelings, to the repressed, unfulfilled *intention* itself, or to the resulting feelings. Charge results in *unwanted feelings,* resistance, disordered thinking, emotional or psychosomatic pain and/or *aberrant behavior.*

Chart Method of Case Planning: *Case planning* by lining up against the client's issues those *viewing techniques* likely to be helpful in resolving each issue.

Checklist: A *viewing method* consisting of a linear sequence of actions, all of which are done in a prescribed order. A checklist is used to accomplish a specific purpose, such as to reduce *charge* from a *traumatic incident*, and is carried to an *end point*.

Chronic Upset: An *upset* that recurs often or that exists continually over a long period of time.

Co-Facilitation: A partnership between two or more *persons*, in which they alternate being *facilitator* and *viewer* for each other, so that both can get help and both can have the experience of helping. Sometimes it is best to have more than two and use a "round robin" schedule.

Collection: A list of different *viewing techniques* designed to address thoroughly a particular kind of long-term issue. The collection contains those techniques that have been found to work best for that issue. The *technical director* (or the *facilitator* acting as technical director) can use a collection to add steps to a *case plan* for a *viewer* by selecting those techniques in the collection that are appropriate to that particular viewer and putting them in the order that is best for that viewer. The list of steps so generated is used until an *end point* on the issue is achieved. Compare *program*.

Comment: A casual remark by the *viewer* that is not of great concern to them and therefore does not require more than a simple *acknowledgment* in order for them to return to the *viewing technique* they have been doing. Compare *concern*.

Commitment: An act of *assent* consisting of a decision to make an *intention*.. A decision to *begin to engage* in an *activity*. Compare *acceptance*.

Communication: The transfer of a *token* (such as a word, phrase, or symbol) from one *person* to another, where the *thing* (_concept_ or _phenomenon_) that the receiver *interprets* the token as representing is the same as the *thing* that the originator intended to convey by using the token.

Communication Cycle: An *activity cycle* that starts when one *person* attempts to communicate to another. It ends when the originator knows that their communication has been *comprehended* by the receiver, or when they give up the attempt to communicate. Compare *instruction cycle*.

Communication Exercises (CEs): Exercises intended to improve communication skills, in which the various basic components of communication (*confronting*, delivering a communication, *acknowledging*, etc.) are practiced to a point of expertise.

Communication Section: A section of the *Curriculum* that concerns itself with difficulties with and charge on the issue of *communication*.

Communion: A combination of *communication*, *comprehension*, and *affection* that characterizes a *person*'s relationship with another person. These three factors tend to form an ascending triad: more communication leads to more comprehension and more affection, more comprehension leads to more affection and more communication, and more affection leads to more communication and more comprehension. On the other hand, a drop in one of the three components causes a drop in the other two and in communion itself. When this drop happens suddenly, we call it an *upset*. The easiest entry point to this triad is through *communication*. Compare *power*.

Comparing: One of the basic actions that a *viewer* is asked to do in *viewing*. It is the act of describing the relationship between two *person*s or *things*.

Completing a Cycle: Since an *activity cycle* depends, for its existence, on the existence of an *intention*, the cycle is complete when the intention is either fulfilled or unmade. Failing to complete cycles clutters up a *person*'s "now" with too many ongoing activities happening at the same time.

Comprehension: The act of correctly identifying the *concept* or experience that the originator of a *communication* intends to convey. The sharing of experience that occurs when communication is successful. Comprehension is the result of communication. It need not involve agreement. Compare *understanding*.

CON (Used in *Unstacking*): The quality of being in opposition to, against, or on the opposite side to the *viewer* in a conflict, either now or from a past viewpoint. If the viewer is a firefighter, the *identity* "an arsonist" might be a CON identity for them.

Conceiving: The act of creating a concept.

Concept: A *thing* that may or may not exist, to which a symbol or statement may refer. An idea or thought, not a mental picture or *phenomenon*. It may be represented by a symbol, but it is not the symbol.

Conceptual Skill: The ability to use *concepts* to *understand* or to create other concepts.

Concern: A *viewer's* communication that, unlike a mere *comment*, requires more than a simple *acknowledgment* in order for the viewer to feel comfortable about returning to the *viewing technique* they were working on. A viewer with a concern cannot readily comply with the *viewing instruction* they have been given until the concern has been appropriately addressed.

Conclusion: A *fact* arrived at from *assumptions* or from *data* by the process of *understanding* (*interpreting* and *assenting* to an interpretation of) the data.

Concurrence: An agreement between two or more *persons* that one or more *things* exist, a shared *assent* to those *things*. There are various degrees of concurrence, depending on how much is shared.

Condition: The degree of *success* a *person* is having in a given *activity*.

Conditioning: The creation of *automatisms*. Conditioning is based on *deficiency motivation*, an attempt to avoid or relieve *pain* or discomfort. In a conditioning situation, a *person* has a "choice" of performing the conditioned action or experiencing pain or discomfort and, if the pain is not confrontable, the choice has to be to act. A series of such experiences creates an *automatism*. Compare *learning*.

Confront (noun): The ability to face up to something or someone or to *things* or people in general, the ability to be *aware* of them,

Confront (verb): To face or pay attention to something or someone without necessarily doing anything else. Compare *handle*.

Congruity: The tendency of different parts of a *person's* world to align with each other, to work together harmoniously to further the *intentions* of the person. The absence of inconsistency or conflict, either with the person's intentions or with each other, between the parts of a person's world.

Consciousness: See *power*.

Consideration: The act of considering. Also, the product of an act of considering, i.e., a *judgment* that a certain *concept* is *true*, false, or has a certain probability.

Considering: The action of coming to decide whether to convert a *concept* into a *fact* by giving *assent* to it, to convert it into an unreality by *dissenting* from it, or to convert it into a probability by giving it something between full assent and full dissent. In considering, one weighs the pros and cons of accepting a concept, based on the principles of organizing experience to maximize personal *power* and *communion*, and then finally decides or determines that it is factual, probable, improbable, or non-factual.

Consultant: A role adopted by an *Applied Metapsychology* practitioner engaged in working out life strategies with a client. A *consultation* follows the *Rules of Consultation*, which differ in some ways from the *Rules of Facilitation*.

Consultation: A way of helping another when they need assistance in dealing with the outer world, rather than the inner world of mind and emotions. In consultation, the practitioner works with the client to formulate an *action plan* to address a specific situation, or one designed to address life more comprehensively, and to assist the client in carrying it out. Compare *facilitation*.

Consultation Session: A *session* in which consultation occurs. Compare *viewing session*.

Continual Misdeeds: Harmful acts that are done repeatedly or continually. One has difficulty allowing oneself to improve when one is continually committing *misdeeds*.

Control: The ability to perform *creative actions* on the world or some part of it. Control is on the *person* side of the *person-world polarity*. The counterpart on the world side is *order*.

Counter-Intention: The *intention* that some *thing* not exist. The *thing* opposed may be an *object*, an *event*, a *situation*, or another intention.

Creation: A *creative action*. Also, the product of such an action.

Creative: A directionality toward the world from the *person*. Giving, rather than receiving. Pushing out, rather than pulling in. Compare *receptive*.

Creative Action: The action of creating a *fact*, *phenomenon*, or *concept*, of putting a *thing* out into the world or producing a change in the world. Basic creative actions include *picturing*, *conceiving*, and *positing*. Compare *receptive action*.

Creative Technique: A *viewing technique* in which the *viewer* is asked to perform one or more *creative action*s, such as visualizing an event or *situation*.

Creativity: The ability to engage in *creative actions*; the ability to bring *things* into existence.

Crossflow: The causation of some kind of effect between two or more *persons*, or between one or more persons and one or more *things*, as viewed by another person who is not directly involved. See *flow*.

Current Situation: The present *situation* or environment the client finds themselves in, in a certain area or *domain* or in life in general. Compare *ideal situation*.

Curricular Action: An action or *viewing technique* that is part of person's *Curriculum*. Compare *remedy*.

Curriculum (Ability Enhancement Viewing Curriculum): A long general *case plan* broken down into eight sections, which can be customized for each individual *viewer*. The curriculum gives the sequence of *techniques* designed to gradually increase a viewer's *abilities* by removing *charge* from the *case*, and by exercising life *skills* the viewer already has in order to improve the viewer's command over these skills. The Curriculum uses *discovery* mode.

Cycle: See *activity cycle*.

Danger: A *condition* in which one is faced with an overwhelming threat with which one feels one may not be able to cope. One's impulse is to flee, to disengage, but one has not yet done so. The corresponding emotion on the *person* side of the *person-world polarity* is Fear.

Datum (plural: data): Something that is "given" to a *person*, in other words *accepted* by them. A datum is either a *phenomenon* or a *fact*. Compare *conclusion*.

Deactivation: A situation in which, because of passage of time, change of environment, or some other reason (such as the application of a *viewing technique*), an *active* sequence, *traumatic incident*, or *disturbance* becomes *inactive*. The undoing of activation. The *charge* may still be present, but in an inactive state. When an area of *emotional charge* has dropped or is dropping out of a triggered state; the emotional charge is still in existence, ready to perhaps be triggered another time, but it is not currently impinging on the *viewer's* consciousness.

Debilitation: A relative absence of *power* (*drive, control,* and *understanding*) with respect to *things*. It forms a descending triad, with less drive leading to less control and understanding, less control leading to less drive and understanding, and less understanding leading to less control and drive.

Debug List: A list containing the most likely errors or unwanted *conditions* that can exist in a particular *session*, designed to find the source of a problem and get it resolved so that the session can be completed successfully. Sometimes a debug list can be handled as an *assessment list*.

Declaration: A statement of fact, delivered as a communication to another *person* or persons, with the *intention* that they *assent* to it.

Deficiency Motivation: A term used by Abraham Maslow to refer to the pursuit of *negative pleasures*, such as quenching thirst, scratching an itch, or relieving sexual tension. It is a motivation to escape from an uncomfortable situation, to obtain *relief*.

Delusion: A *falsehood* introduced in the act of *repression* in order to help hide the repressed material. See also *fixed idea, anesthetic idea*.

Denial: A refusal to accept an obvious *interpretation* of a *datum* as *true*. A failure to accept as a *fact* a *concept* that would be accepted if it were not for an inability or unwillingness to *confront*.

Describing: One of the basic actions a *viewer* is asked to do in *viewing*, consisting of viewing and communicating the characteristics of what is viewed.

Descriptive Item: An *item* that describes a specific *traumatic incident*, as opposed to a thematic item or *theme*, which describes a category of trauma. See also *FESAPs*.

Desire: *Affinity* directed toward *things*. An impulse toward *having* or continuing to *have* a *thing*. Compare *Affection*.

Detour: A necessary deviation from a technique or *program*, designed to handle an emergent situation that the current technique or program is not capable of handling. Although it is a deviation, it is designed specifically to take one around an obstacle and to return one to the main route as soon as possible. Compare *sidetrack*.

Dichotomy (in *Unstacking*): A special kind of *problem* which is of great significance to a *person* because it concerns that which is of paramount importance for them: a *basic goal* and the survival of a *basic identity*. A dichotomy exists when this basic identity (*proponent*) is opposed by another major identity (*opponent*) with its own basic goal that opposes the proponent's *goal*. See also *stack*.

Dilemma: A conflict between two or more of a *person's* current *intentions*.

Dimension: A quality of a *world* that permits the separation of its component parts.

Directed Unawareness: See *Repression*.

Disability: A personal characteristic or situation that lowers a *person's* level of *power* or *communion*.

Disaffection: *Aversion* directed toward a *person*. The characteristic of being unwilling to be close to another person, to share a space or viewpoint with them. It is an impulse toward *alienation*. A high degree of disaffection is "hatred".

Discharge: The bringing to *awareness* of the contents of a *traumatic incident*, including any *intentions* contained in it, with a consequent fulfillment or cancellation of the intentions and a movement of the traumatic incident out of the present into the past as a completed (and no longer traumatic) incident which no longer contains *charge* and cannot be *activated*. Compare *deactivation*.

Discharge by Inspection: A *discharge* that occurs as soon as an *item* is spotted.

Discovery: The mode of *facilitation* that selectively *reactivates*, addresses and *discharges* areas not currently *activated* for the purpose of increasing the *viewer's ability* and stabilizing the *person* at a higher level of functioning, as well as exercising abilities the person innately has, in order to bring them more under the person's command. Compare *unburdening*.

Disengaged (from viewing): The condition in which the *viewer* is either not interested in their *case*, not willing to talk to the *facilitator* about it, not willing or able to comply with *viewing instructions*, or some combination of the above. In other words, the viewer is disengaged from *viewing* when the *instruction channel*, the *viewing channel*, or the *report channel* are not functioning properly.

Disengagement: The act of moving away from a particular *identity* or *activity*, of assigning it less importance, of discontinuing it.

Dissent: The action of disagreeing, of saying "no" to a *concept*. It is one possible outcome of *considering*, the other possibilities being *assent* and assignment of a probability. Dissent is really only a form of assent. To dissent with the concept "a red car in front of my house" is to assent to the obverse concept "no red car in front of my house".

Dissonance: A lack of mental harmony. Dissonance is what corresponds, on the *person* side of the *person-world polarity*, to *incongruity* on the world side.

Disturbance: A subject, *situation*, or *item* that is currently in a state of *reactivation*. Such items include *upsets, problems, withholds, misdeeds*, and *traumatic incidents*. A disturbance is an area of *charge* on which the *viewer* has their attention fixed. This area may or may not be one of the major issues that were supposed to be addressed in the *session*. Nevertheless, it needs to be handled first by *unburdening* (at the start of a session or as part of a *remedial* plan) so that the viewer can free their attention from the disturbance and thus be ready for the *major action* of the session.

Disturbance Handling: The handling of *disturbances*, done at the beginning of a *session*, to a point where the *viewer*'s attention is relatively unfixed and can be directed toward the *major actions* in the *session agenda*. Disturbances can be handled when they (rarely) come up during a session's *major action*. A further application of Disturbance Handling is when they are used as a major action in themselves, being addressed to the *flows* in life in general, or addressed to a particular relationship.

Domain: A sphere of *responsibility*. There are six domains: self, *intimates*, groups, humankind, all life, and the Infinite. These domains are concentric; each successive domain contains the previous ones, with the self at the center. Each domain has a subjective or mental side and an objective or physical side, reflecting the *polar* relationship between *person* and *world*.

Domain Assessment: An *exploring* of a *viewer's domains* as an *assessment* to find charged *items* to address using various *viewing techniques*.

Domain Exploration Program: A systematic investigation of the *domains*, using *Exploration* as a *viewing technique*.

Drive: The general capacity to desire. A "lust for life". A *person* with a great deal of drive is capable of having many desires and strong ones; a person with little drive doesn't care much about things. Drive is an essential ingredient (along with *ability*) of *power*. Without drive, a person, however able, is not powerful.

Drudgery: A *condition* in which one feels one is fighting one's environment. One is trying very hard to succeed in an *activity*, not making adequate progress, and not enjoying it. The corresponding emotional level is between Anger and *Ambivalence*. "Frustration" might describe the general frame of mind. One feels trapped in one's situation, with little hope of improvement. One's strategy is to resist, to use force, and to fight back. One becomes less productive and tends to develop a backlog of *incomplete cycles*.

Earlier Starting Point: A *viewing instruction* in *TIR* in which one asks for an earlier start to an incident.

Ego Strength: The strength of a personality to maintain itself. Ego strength comes from the essence of the *person*, whether you consider that to be of the nature of personality, *mind*, or spirit. Strength requires flexibility. People with good ego strength are able to maintain their own points of view, to tolerate differing points of view from other people, to be objective, and to change their own minds about something as they learn and gain experience.

Emergency: In a *condition* of Emergency, one is constantly coping with immediate threats. One is close to being overwhelmed and building up major backlogs (*incomplete cycles*) because one does not have time to handle routine chores. One tries to be hyper-alert, to attend compulsively and indiscriminately to every detail in the environment that seems to be a threat, and to ignore or neglect other things that, while still needing attention, are less immediately threatening. One is not so severely under threat that one feels one has to run away. Rather, one's attention is drawn compulsively to the threat, and one loses sight of the importance of other things. The emotional level corresponding to Emergency is Anxiety.

Emotional Charge: See *Charge*.

Emotional Scale: A spectrum of different emotions felt by people as they encounter varying degrees of success or failure in an activity or have varying degrees of affinity or aversion for something or someone; A continuum of emotions, ranked in increasing order of adaptiveness and success, between Apathy (corresponding to *Final Failure*) and Elation (corresponding to *Final Success*). Also see *Table of Attitudes*.

Empowerment: The combination of *pleasure, order,* and *heuristics* that the *person* attempts to create in and receive from their world. It is the counterpart, on the *world* side of the *person-world polarity*, to *power* on the person side.

End Point: The point at which the *cycle* connected with an *activity* has been successfully completed. This is the point at which the activity should be ended. It is manifested by a set of phenomena that indicate the successful termination of the activity. These *indicators* vary from activity to activity. In *viewing*, an end point is the point at which a *viewing technique* is completed. Here, it consists of *extroversion* of the *viewer's* attention, positive or *very positive indicators*, and often a *realization* of some kind. Compare *flat point*.

Engaged (in *viewing*): The state in which the *viewer* is interested in their *charged* issues, willing to talk to the *facilitator* about them, and willing to follow *viewing instructions*. The opposite condition is one in which the viewer is *disengaged*: not interested in their issues, not willing to talk to the facilitator about them, or not willing to follow instructions. When the *instruction channel*, *viewing channel*, and *report channel* are in full operation, a *person* is well engaged in viewing,

Engagement: The degree to which a *person* assumes an *identity*, or the importance they place on a particular activity. Engagement is "how much of oneself one puts into" an *activity* or identity.

Engagement Program: A series of steps intended to help a *person* become more *engaged* in an *activity*.

Entity: See *thing*.

Environment: The *person's* entire world, including the physical world, their body, and their *mind*. The *viewer's* mind is part of their environment, not part of the viewer. Also, a part of the viewer's world that is close by, such as the *facilitation* room.

Ethics: Control of *intention*; intending to intend; the ability to choose amongst different intentions, *identity*, and *activities* in order to produce the optimum result across the *domains*. A *person* must have *versatility* in order to be ethical.

Evaluation: An *assertion* that something or someone is good or bad. *Viewers* must make their own evaluations in a *viewing session*. The *facilitator* must not evaluate *for* them. Compare *interpreting*.

Event: A *thing* that is described as something that is happening. A process, rather than an *object* or a *situation*.

Evil: That which is *counter-intended*. Compare *good*.

Existence: From a *person-centered viewpoint*, the quality of being a *phenomenon*, *fact*, or *concept* in a *person's world*.

Exploration: A *viewing technique* using the exploring *method*, designed to be taken to its own *end point* with respect to a specific *item* or issue.

Exploring: A *method* used in *viewing* that is used in only one *technique*: Exploration. Unlike *TIR* or a *sequential unlayering* technique such as *Unblocking*, exploring has no set viewing instructions. It can be used to find *items* to address and to explore areas of *charge* and *interest* so as to write effective *case plans* for them.

Extroversion: Looking outward. Looking toward the *world* side of the *person-world polarity*. In *viewing*, the action of a *viewer's* attention moving from inward to outward, or from the past to the present. Extroversion is an indicator of an *end point*. Compare *introversion*.

Facilitation: The act of helping another to perform the actions of *viewing*. In facilitation, the *facilitator* asks the *viewer* to perform an action or answer a question (often repetitively), the viewer does the action or answers the question, and the facilitator acknowledges the viewer for so doing.

Facilitator: A *person* who helps another to perform the actions of *viewing*. The facilitator's function is to help the *viewer* view their world and thereby to alleviate the *charge* and *aberration* contained therein.

Fact: A *thing* that exists for a *person* at a certain moment but cannot be *perceived*. A *concept* that is accepted as real; a concept to which a person gives *assent*.

Factuality: (of a *concept*) The condition of being *assented* to or agreed with by a *person*. *Truth*.

Failure: A *condition* in which a *person* realizes that they are not being *successful* in carrying out an *intention* or engaging in an *activity*. At the point of Failure, the person begins to disengage from the activity. Emotions corresponding to Failure are Grief_and_Apathy.

Faith: A degree of certainty that is sufficient for action. Faith usually falls short of total certainty, but it is the point at which we feel we can cease *considering* something and begin acting.

False Belief: A belief based on unawareness of *things* with which it is *incongruent*.

FESAPs: Short for Feelings, Emotions, Sensations, Attitudes, and Pains, in other words, *themes* that can be addressed in *Thematic TIR*.

Final Failure: A degree of failure that mandates complete *disengagement* from an *activity*.

Final Success: The fulfillment of an *intention*, leading to a *disengagement* from the intended *activity*. The corresponding emotion is Elation.

First Consideration: The first decision a *person* makes on a particular topic. This *consideration* therefore cannot be a contradiction of an earlier consideration on the same subject. It is possible, however, for the person to add a layer of *delusion* on top of the first consideration—a *second consideration* that is *incongruent* with the first, then to add a third that is incongruent with the second, and so forth.

Fixed Goal: A *goal* that a *person* has trouble letting go of.

Fixed Idea: A *concept* that is adhered to because it serves to make it unnecessary for the *viewer* to *confront* something such as a painful situation, a confusion, or a *problem*, or because it serves to hold a *fixed identity* in place and thus seems important for the "survival" of that identity. A fixed goal leads to a fixed identity, and a fixed identity has fixed ideas that hold it in place. To *discharge* and dislodge a fixed goal and identity, it is usually necessary to address and discharge the fixed ideas that go along with it. See *anesthetic idea*.

Fixed Identity: An *identity* a *person* has assumed in an effort to avoid pain or unpleasantness, one which the person does not feel completely free to give up.

Flat: Of a *technique* or *item*, to come to a point of *no change* or no further *charge* available at that time. Also, in *Communication Exercise* 3, when a student no longer reacts to a *button*, it is said to be "flat".

Flat Point: A point at which no more *charge* is currently available, no change is occurring, and the *viewer* is no longer interested in continuing, though a full *end point* has not been attained.

Flattened : 1. Of a *button* in *Communication Exercise* 3: no longer eliciting a *reaction* from the student. 2. Of a *viewing technique*: no longer causing change in the *viewer*.

Flow: A directionality of causation between *persons* or between persons and *things*. See *inflow, outflow, crossflow,* and *reflexive flow.*

Force: Something that has coercive power because it involves things that are difficult to *confront*. In *viewing*, you are generally trying to have the *viewer* find and handle force, rather than *significance*.

Future TIR (FTIR): A special application of *TIR* to remove *charge* from future events, whether probable or improbable, that the *viewer* is concerned about.

General TIR: A section of the *Curriculum* in which *TIR* is used to handle *items* that are not currently *activated* or areas of life that are not currently bothering the *viewer*. Its intent is to prevent future activation and difficulties and to remove *charge* from the *case* generally and thoroughly.

Get the Idea (GTI): A *technique* useful in the rapid "unsticking" of *fixed ideas*.

Goal: an *intention* that ends when its *objective* is achieved. Compare *purpose*.

Good: From a *person-centered viewpoint*, that which aids in the fulfillment of the *person's intentions*. Compare *evil*.

Good Deed: An action that aligns with the major *intentions* of the majority of people affected by the action. Compare *misdeed*.

Great Person Syndrome: The condition of being fixed in a successful, over-extended or high status *identity* to avoid the pain of being unsuccessful.

Grounding Techniques: Relatively brief *techniques* used as *remedies* to assist a *person* in reaching a more comfortable state by directing *attention* to objects in the present environment. Grounding techniques are palliative, and do not necessarily cause significant change in the person's condition..

Handle: To direct *creative actions* toward something. Compare *confront*.

Happiness: The *knowledge* that one is being successful at fulfilling one's *intentions*. The subjective state that corresponds to the progressive attainment of *success*.

Harm: Actions that people view as opposing their *intentions*. Compare *help*.

Having: The ability to be causative over (to have *access* to or *influence* on) a *thing*.

Help: Actions that people view as furthering their *intentions*. Compare *harm*.

Help and Control Section: That section of the *Curriculum* that is concerned with handling the *viewer's charge* on the subjects of help and *control*.

Heuristic: Tending to promote *learning* or *understanding*. School should be a heuristic environment.

Heuristics: The quality of a world or part of a world by virtue of which it promotes *learning* or greater *understanding*. Heuristics is the counterpart, on the *world* side of the *person-world polarity*, to *understanding* on the *person* side.

Hierarchy of Intentions and Identities: *Intentions* have a hierarchical "tree" structure. One or more junior intentions tend to promote the fulfillment of a senior one; one or more senior intentions may tend to promote an even more senior intention, and so forth. Corresponding to this hierarchy is a hierarchy of *identities*, since each intention, even a lower-level one, has a corresponding identity by which it can be fulfilled.

Ideal Situation: The optimal state of affairs attainable in the area you are addressing, a statement of what you are trying to bring about in the real world by pursuing your *goal* or *purpose*.

Identity: A package of viewpoints, tools, and *abilities* that can be incorporated as part of the self in order to fulfill an *intention*. Any identity has a ruling intention—the intention for which the identity was assumed. Thus, for instance, to build things out of wood one must assume the identity of a carpenter. An identity must be a role one can play, not just a *concept*. One can also have a *social identity*.

Inactive: An inactive *sequence* or *traumatic incident* is one that (because of the passage of time, a change of environment, or some other reason) is not easily *triggered*. Compare *active*.

Incident: A finite period of time defined by a specific *activity cycle*.

Incomplete Cycle: An *activity* that is ongoing and occupies a *person's* "now" because its ruling *intention* has neither been fulfilled nor unmade.

Incongruity: An incompatibility, conflict, or misalignment between two elements of a *person's* world. It is what corresponds, on the *world* side of the *person-world polarity*, to *dissonance* on the person side. The opposite of *alignment*.

Indication: A "pointing out" of something. If you say. "Look, the sun is shining" you have indicated that fact. If you turn on the left turn signal in your car, that is an indication of your intention to turn left. With respect to a viewer's case, an indication is a deliberate *assertion* about something related to the *person's case*, personality, or *situation*. In *facilitation*, an indication must only be given as an agreement with something the viewer already *knows* consciously. *Wrong indications* may be a major source of difficulty, if given in or out of a *viewing session*.

Indicator: Something that shows how well or poorly an *activity* is going. In *viewing, Positive indicators* include *extroversion, viewer* looking brighter, smiles, laughter, and *realizations*. *Negative indicators* include any viewer manifestations of dissatisfaction with the *session* or *facilitator, disengagement* from the session, viewer looking pale, etc.

Inflow: The receipt of an effect by a *person* from a *thing* or another person.

Influence: The ability to be causative creatively with respect to something. Also, (as a verb) to exercise such causative *creativity*. *Access* and *influence* are the two forms of *having* (*receptive* and *creative*, respectively).

In-Session Unburdening: Handling of *disturbances* that arise in the middle of a *session*.

Insight: A coming to *awareness* of an *underlying truth*.

Instruction: See *Viewing Instruction*.

Instruction Channel: In a *session*, the channel along which the *viewer* receives *viewing instructions*. Compare *viewing channel, report channel*.

Instruction Cycle: A *cycle* created when one *person* gives an instruction to one or more other people. It is complete when the person or people to whom the instruction was given comply with the instruction and the issuer of the instruction is aware of that fact, or when they end the *intention* by ceasing to try to get compliance.

Integrative Learning: The second phase of the *learning cycle* in which one verifies *data* that have been received and fits the data in with the rest of one's belief system.

Integrity: *Congruity* of *intention* and *identity*.

Intelligibility: The quality of something by virtue of which it can be understood by a *person*. It is the counterpart, on the *world* side of the *person-world polarity*, to *understanding* on the person side.

Intention: A *goal* or *purpose*. An impulse toward causation. The part of an *action* that lies closest to the *person*. A clear, strong intention with no admixture of *counter-intention* usually results in the successful completion of a *cycle*. A common cause of failure is the absence of a sufficiently strong intention or the presence of counter-intentions. One's degree of *power*, consciousness, or intention might be quantified as a certain amount of intention that is available to be used at any given time. If some of the available intention is "used up" in ongoing activities, one has less intention available to take on new *activities* or to succeed in existing activities. See also *attention, volition*.

Interest: Directed *attention*. Interest can be either other-directed or intentionally self-directed. When a *facilitator* asks a *viewer* whether the viewer is interested in something, they are checking for other-directed interest: a feeling of having one's attention attracted to something because of a sense of its importance, a felt desire to attend to something and reduce its *emotional charge*. In the *Communication Exercises*, the student learns to generate self-directed interest.

Interest Rating: An interest rating is a number that a *viewer* can assign to each *item* or issue they raise in an intake or update *interview*, based on the amount of interest they have in that issue. The degree of interest can range from "0", meaning no interest to "10", meaning very high interest. Distress can be similarly rated. Viewer interest level is more important than distress level, however.

Interpreting: Finding a meaning, significance, or explanation a certain *datum* might refer to or imply, thereby arriving at a *concept*. An interpretation is not a *fact* until and unless it has been *considered, verified*, and *assented* to. In *viewing sessions, facilitators* do not make interpretations *for* their *viewers*. Viewers make their own interpretations and arrive at their own insights.

Interview: An inquiry into a *viewer's* life, frequently quite detailed and extensive, during which the *facilitator explores* various potentially *charged* areas in order to determine what issues the viewer has had in the past and what the viewer's *attention* is currently focused on.

Intimates: People who are close friends, lovers, or family members. This is the second *domain*.

Introspection: Looking toward the *mind* rather than toward the physical universe. A *person* or *identity* cannot, however, look "inside" itself.

Introversion: Used in the context of *viewing* to mean the action and fact of a *viewer's attention* moving inward toward the *mind*, rather than toward the outer world. In life this can be a bad sign: "Hearing criticism of her character caused her to introvert painfully." During a *session* there is nothing wrong with a viewer's attention moving inward. Without this, no useful work gets done. Compare *extroversion*.

Introvert: to move someone's attention inward toward the *mind* rather than outward toward the world.

Invalidation: Attributing a negative value or invalidity to something or someone. Also, saying or implying to others that they are bad people or that their beliefs or perceptions are false.

Item: 1. A *thing* or topic that is possibly or actually *charged* for the *viewer*. 2. A word, phrase, or sentence that communicates such a *thing* or topic.

Joy: Something that satisfies a *wish* rather than providing the reduction, avoidance, or elimination of *pain* that comes from satisfying a *need*. Compare *relief*.

Judgment: An *assertion* or belief that something or someone is good or bad. The *viewer* makes their own judgments in a *viewing session*. They are not made by the *facilitator*.

Justification: A mechanism for handling the *dissonance* one experiences when one has committed a *misdeed*. Because one does, basically, wish to improve conditions all around, when one finds out that one has worsened them by some misdeed, an *incongruity* exists that can be painful. One means of handling this incongruity is by explaining, to self or others, how one's action was not really a misdeed. This explanation can then serve as a rationale for future similar misdeeds.

Knowing: The *having* of a fact.

Learning: The acquisition of knowledge or *skill* by the *learning cycle*. Compare *conditioning*.

Learning Cycle: The way in which a *person* acquires new knowledge. The *cycle* by which a person moves from a *datum* or data to a new *thing*. The learning cycle has two phases: a receptive phase, in which one acquires new data and an integrative phase in which one verifies the data, notices its implications, and fits it in with the rest of one's belief system. A great deal has been written about this subject under the heading of the laws of deduction and induction.

Life Coaching: The work done by a *facilitator* acting as a *consultant* to help the client to address issues via actual in-life actions.

Life Coaching Schema Workshop: A workshop that teaches a systematic approach to helping clients examine and streamline the path to achieving their *goals* and *purposes* in life. It also provides effective tools for helping clients to overcome emotional *charge* accumulated after past failures as well as providing tools for formulating new goals and purposes.

Life Planning: The work a client does to construct and implement a life plan as part of a *Schema Program*.

Life Stress List (LSL): An *assessment list* that is used to deactivate *disturbances*. It is designed to calm and soothe an upset *viewer* or to relieve charge on an area of life.

Life Stress Reduction (LSR): *Viewing* done in preparation for work on the *curriculum* or to return a *viewer* to the curriculum after a *detour* therefrom. Life Stress Reduction addresses issues on which the viewer's *attention* is already fixed and reduces *charge* on these issues so that the amount of *stress* the viewer is suffering from is reduced. Although Life Stress Reduction often produces spectacular relief, it is only the first major step in a complete *case* handling. It is best regarded as a preparation for a more thoroughgoing approach to the viewer's *case*, i.e., for the *Curriculum*.

Life Stress Reduction Workshop. (LSRW): A second-level *AMP* workshop that teaches Life Stress Reduction techniques. The LSRW and the *TIR-Expanded Applications* workshops expand a *TIR Workshop* graduate's range of tools and professional skills, allowing the student to go beyond addressing *traumatic incidents* to effectively address a wider variety of human concerns and issues. The TIR Workshop is a prerequisite for both.

Live: Of an *item*: one that carries *charge* and lies just below the *awareness threshold* and thus is accessible to the *viewer*. Such an item will attract the viewer's *interest*.

Long-term Trauma Handling (LTT): A technique for addressing traumatic periods of life that are too lengthy for *TIR*.

Loop: An example of the *unlayering method* in which a single question or set of questions are asked repeatedly until an *end point* is reached.

Major Action: A *program* or *technique*, contained in the *case plan* and the *session agenda*, that is done as part of the *body of a session*.

Mass: The quality of an *object* that causes it to resist translation (change of location). Also, the presence of *phenomena* (as in study), as opposed to *concepts* or *facts*. Compare *significance*.

Medical Model: The concept that people who are having trouble in life are therefore "sick" and must be treated by a doctor or para-medical person, and that the difficulties such a person encounters in life constitute, or are indicative of, a "disease" that has to be "cured" in a medical or quasi-medical way. *Applied Metapsychology* does not follow the medical model.

Memory Enhancement Section: The section of the *Curriculum* that is concerned with helping the *viewer* recover the ability to contact the past easily. *Objective* and *subjective techniques* used in *Life Stress Reduction* and in the *Help and Control Section* enabled the viewer to contact the present with ease and to perform actions freely in the present. The next step is for the viewer to learn to contact and handle the past with equal facility.

Memory Technique: A *receptive, subjective viewing technique* in which the *viewer* contacts past, non-traumatic incidents. In using a memory technique, viewers do not try to re-experience the past incident. They only make contact with it. Memory techniques improve a *person's* memory for, and familiarity with, the past.

Metapsychology: The study of the individual *person* and their experience, as seen from their point of view. Metapsychology is the study of the person and their *abilities*, the origin, structure, and function of the *mind*, and the relationship between person, mind, and physical universe. It is the discipline that unifies mental and physical experience; it seeks to discover the rules that apply to both. Central to metapsychology is a study of how the person, the mind, and the *world* are seen from a *"person-centered" viewpoint* in the absence of any external viewpoint or *judgments*.

Metapsychology picks up where psychology, as the science of *behavior*, leaves off. Hence the name "metapsychology" has the correct connotation of being a study that goes "beyond" psychology, beyond the study of behavior to the study of that which behaves: the person themself, and the person's *perceptual*, *conceptual*, and *creative* activity, as distinguished from the actions of the *body*. In this sense, "metapsychology" restores the original meaning of "psychology" as "the study of the psyche, or spirit", and *Applied Metapsychology* reflects the perennial common goal of therapies, religions, and traditional philosophies, whether one calls this goal the attainment of sanity, of enlightenment, of *happiness*, or of wisdom,.

Method: A pattern of a set of similar *viewing techniques*. Methods in viewing include *exploring, unlayering, loop, selecting, checklist,* and *assessment list*. The *exploring* method contains just one technique: *Exploration*, and *selecting* contains only one technique: *Selection*. The other methods are each used in many different viewing techniques.

Mind: The set of *things* that exist for a *person* but that, under ordinary circumstances, other people cannot be *aware* of or act upon directly. It is that person's set of "private" *things*, that person's "private" *world*, the part that is closest to the person. The mind, however, is still part of a person's *environment*, not part of the person. Mental actions, *creative* or *receptive*, are not experienced by the person as being mediated through the *body*.

Misconception: A word, phrase, symbol, or sentence for which there appears to be no corresponding *concept* or for which the corresponding concept received is not that intended by the originator of the *communication* containing that word, phrase, symbol, or sentence.

Misdeed: An action that runs counter to the individual's own *moral* or *ethical* code.

MO: See *modus operandi*.

Modus Operandi (MO): A habitual, often complex, pattern of *behavior*. It is how one *actually* behaves, as distinguished from how one feels one *should* behave, according to one's own moral code or set of personal policies. Compare *policy*.

Morals: Group *policies* that are based on an unknown rationale, i.e., whose relationship to the stated intentions of the group is unknown. A moral code, having an implicit or unexamined rationale, may "take on a life of its own". Perhaps the rationale was once stated explicitly, but, the rationale having been lost, the *policy* has remained. Thus the policy may appear to be intrinsically right, since no reason has been given for it, so it may become permanently inscribed as a moral imperative. There is, perhaps, a feeling of absolute rightness about it that is unexamined, yet it may, nonetheless, be firmly agreed upon by the members of a group. Adherence to morality ultimately rests on the notion (sometimes ill-thought-out or outmoded) that a breach of a group moral code is more or less automatically guaranteed to be against the interests of the group. Compare *ethics*.

Multi-Determinism: The consideration that one shares responsibility for the *intentions* and actions of other *persons* involved in a certain situation. See also *other-determinism, self-determinism*.

Negative Feeling: A feeling, emotion, sensation, attitude, or pain that is negative or unwanted, caused by unresolved *charge*.

Negative Indicator: A phenomenon that indicates that a person is not being successful in carrying out some activity. A bad grade in school, or shortness of breath in a heart patient, are bad indicators. *Viewer* lack of *engagement* is a negative indicator in *viewing*. Negative feelings are often bad indicators.

Negative Pleasure: See *relief*.

Need: A *desire* for something the absence of which would be experienced as painful to the *person*. A need is satisfied by something that is a *relief*. Compare *wish*.

Net: See *Traumatic Incident Network*.

No Change: One of the *phenomena* that indicate that an *end point* has been reached in a *viewing technique*. This is when a technique has been applied for a period of time without any particular changes occurring. It is one of the lighter or weaker indications that a technique should be stopped.

Non-Zero-Sum Game An activity that does not call for winners and losers; an activity where, at least in theory, everyone could succeed. *Multi-determined* people play non-zero-sum games.

Normal: A *condition* in which a *person* feels basically content with, though unexcited about, an activity. The natural impulse at this level is to keep doing what one is doing and not to change things. In this condition, everything tends to go smoothly. The person gets along well with family members, fellow workers, or companions and acts in an adequate, conscientious, if uninspired, manner. Left to their own devices, people in a Normal condition will remain in that condition indefinitely. The corresponding emotional level is Contentment or Complacency.

OBE: See *out-of-body experience*.

Object (in experience): A discrete, self-contained *thing*, like a table or chair, as opposed to an *event* or *situation*.

Object: (In *viewing*) A *person* or *thing* that can be acted upon, communicated to, or perceived. It is a *thing* or person you can relate to directly, not a mere *concept* or relationship. A mother, a rabbit, and a typewriter are all objects. Motherhood, wildness, and typography are not objects but *significances*.

Objective (adjective): Being on or toward the *world* side of the *person-world polarity*.

Objective (noun): The *situation* at which a *goal* or *purpose* aims.

Objective Technique: A *technique* used in *viewing* that directs a *viewer's attention* toward physical objects. *Receptive* objective techniques include techniques designed to bring the viewer's attention into, and to increase the ability to be *aware* of, the "here and now". Because objective techniques avoid addressing the *mind* directly, they enable the viewer to break through mental barriers in a unique way. They also have the effect of bypassing unwanted habit patterns (*automatisms*) and overly complex ways of thinking. They share with meditation techniques the goal of achieving a kind of simplicity, free of mental *automaticities*. *Creative* objective techniques mainly exercise the ability to control or move the body or other physical objects in various ways. Unlike *grounding techniques*, which are remedies, objective techniques are used to produce *case progress*.

Objectivity: The quality of a *thing* being on the *world* side of the *person-world polarity*.

Occam's Razor: The principle that if two or more explanations of existing data are equally consistent with all these data, one should choose the simplest explanation and the one that depends on the fewest and most modest *assumptions*.

Omitted Data: One of the problems encountered in study, particularly in a "linearly arranged" course. Later sections of such a course usually assume that the student knows and understands the material of earlier sections or earlier courses. If the student does not have these earlier *data*, they cannot continue to learn from the course materials.

Omitted Interpretation: A form of *repression*, consisting of a refusal to try to *interpret*, or an inability to interpret a *datum* or to think about it. The *person* is unwilling or unable to make the "obvious" interpretation, the interpretation they would make in the absence of *aversion* and repression.

Opponent: In *Unstacking*, a major_*identity* that opposes a *proponent*—a major identity that the *viewer* is or has assumed in the past. A CON identity in a *stack*.

Order: The condition in a *person*'s world that gives him the opportunity to *control* it. Creative opportunity. It is one of the three principal things a person seeks to create in or receive from his world, the other two being *heuristics* and *pleasure*. Order is the counterpart, on the *world* side of the *person-world polarity*, to *control* on the person side. There are three types of order: *simplicity*, *stability*, and *congruity*.

Other-Determinism: The consideration that one is not *responsible* for one's own actions, but that one is responsible for others' actions. See also *multi-determinism, self-determinism*.

Outflow: The *creation* of some kind of effect by the *viewer* on one or more other people or *things*. See *Flow*.

Out-of-Body Experience (OBE): An experience sometimes encountered in *viewing* and in other situations, in which a *person* experiences themself as being located outside the body. Different people report different degrees of ability to *perceive* when having these experiences. This concept gets into the realm of beliefs, as some people experience them as real phenomena, while others regard them as either impossible or a sign of delusion or psychosis. In person-centered work, however, we accept a *viewer's interpretation* of their own experience, regardless of our own beliefs.

Pain: The presence of someone or something to which a *person* has *aversion*, or aversion to a *thing* or person that is present. It can vary from mild discomfort to intense agony. See *physical pain, primary pain, secondary pain, situational pain*.

Past Life Incident: An incident encountered in a *viewing session* that is known not to have occurred in the *viewer's* current lifetime. Whether such incidents are real or imaginary, ignoring or *invalidating* them will usually prevent a resolution of the *charged* material being addressed.

Perceiving: The action of receiving a *phenomenon*, through the senses otherwise.

Person: A living entity or being, as distinct from their body, *mind*, or any *identity* they may *assume* for various purposes. The center of *consciousness* and *action*. That which performs the basic *creative* and *receptive* actions. It is not something people *have*, but what they basically *are*.

Person-Centered Context: A context in which it is implicitly assumed that "I believe that ... " or "I feel that ..." is prefixed to each statement made. All statements made in this context are accepted as valid expressions of the speaker's reality. Their objective truth is irrelevant. *Viewing* takes place in a person-centered context.

Person-Centered Viewpoint: A pragmatic and experiential approach to the study of *persons* and the *worlds* they inhabit. From this viewpoint, we cease talking about some hypothetical world outside of experience and limit ourselves to what each person experiences: their own world. When we talk about *reality* from the person-centered viewpoint, therefore, we must specify whose reality we are referring to. That reality may or may not be shared by anyone else.

Person-World Polarity: The relationship between a *person* and their *world*, which are both connected and separated by the person's *receptive* or *creative* actions. At the one pole there is the person and the *identity* they have *assumed*. At the other pole, there is that which the person *perceives*, that which they *know* or *understand*, that upon which they *act*, and that which they *create* by means of that identity—the totality of what exists for that person at that moment— in other words, that person's *world*.

Phenomenon: A *thing* that is being directly perceived by a *person* or a mental picture they are creating, at a certain moment. If a person is looking at a chair, the chair is a phenomenon for them at that time. Compare *concept, fact*.

Phoniness: *Incongruity* of *intention* and *identity*. We think of people as "phony" when they are pretending to be something they are not or claiming an ability or possessions that they do not really *have*, in order to influence, beguile, or impress people, or to otherwise do something that does not align with the real intentions of that pretended identity. Phoniness is the opposite of *integrity*.

Physical Aversions: "Built-in" *aversions* to certain sensations, including the various sensations called *"physical pain"*, most types of sensory overload (such as overly bright lights or loud noises), and certain other sensations, such as itching, the feeling of hunger, and nausea. They mostly have to do with preserving the *body*. They appear to be inescapable as long as a *person* firmly identifies themself with their body.

Physical Pain: A type of physical sensation to which most people have a *built-in aversion*, including various aches, burning sensations, sharp sensations, and the like. The "painfulness" of physical pain, however, lies in the *person's aversion* to the sensation, not in the sensation itself.

Picturing: The direct *creation* of a mental *phenomenon* by a *person*.

Play: An activity that is done at an emotional level higher than Complacency or in a *condition* higher than *Normal*. The only difference between *work* and *play* is the emotional level at which it is done.

Pleasant TIR: A simplified form of *Basic TIR* applied to past pleasant incidents for the purpose of allowing the *viewer* to re-experience the positive feelings of the event; a light technique used to raise a viewer on the *Emotional Scale* and build *ego strength*. Sometimes used to introduce a viewer to *TIR*.

Pleasure: A *thing* that would satisfy a *person's desire* or desires. It is that which, on the *world* side of the *person-world polarity*, corresponds to desire on the person side. A positive pleasure is a *joy*; a negative pleasure is a *relief*.

Polar Dimension: The *dimension* that extends between the *person* and their *world*. In this dimension, *things* are separated according to their "*objectivity*". *Things* that are less "*objective*" and more "*subjective*" appear closer, in this dimension, to the current *identity* of the person; more "objective" *phenomena* appear more distant. The person, in their current identity, is at the center in this dimension, and it appears that the person always looks "outward", i.e., toward the phenomena they perceive. The polar dimension is linear between the person and each *thing* in their world.

Polarity: 1. A relationship between opposites of being dependent on each other for their existence or of being two aspects of the same thing. The *person* and their *world*, for instance, are opposite sides of the same *person-world polarity*, like the north and south poles of a magnet. The north pole does not exist without the south pole; both are part of the same magnet. 2. The position of a *thing* in the *polar dimension* (degree of *subjectivity* or *objectivity*)..

Policy: A guiding concept or rule adopted or created to align with and further one's *goals* and *purposes* and, when followed, that helps bring *order* and workability to that area of life. A principle one feels one *should* operate on in life. Compare *modus operandi*.

Posit (noun): A *fact* created by the combined actions of *conceiving* and *assenting*.

Posit (verb): To create something by the combined actions of *conceiving* and *assenting*, leading to the *existence* of a *fact*.

Positive Indicator (PI): Something that indicates (implies, means, signifies, or suggests) that a *person* is being *successful* in carrying out some activity. In *viewing*, pleasant emotions, good skin color, and a feeling of *relief* are positive indicators. Compare *negative indicator*.

Positive Recall List: A technique for allowing someone to enjoy pleasant memories.

Post-Traumatic Stress Disorder (PTSD): A condition in which there has been one or more specific, severely *traumatic incidents* that have continued to affect an individual adversely because they are in a state of almost continual or frequent *reactivation*.

Power: A combination of *drive, control,* and *understanding* (or drive and *ability*) that characterizes a *person*'s relationship with the *things* that constitute the person's world. These form a triad, with more drive leading to more control and more understanding, more understanding leading to more drive and more control, and more control leading to more understanding and more drive. Power is the potential a person has for intending things, for making things happen. Power is the degree of "aliveness" or consciousness a person has. It underlies both *awareness* and *creativity* and relates to all the abilities of a person, both *creative* and *receptive*. Power can be expressed as the amount of *intention* a person has to "spend". Compare *empowerment*.

Premise: See *assumption*.

Primary Pain: *Physical* or *situational pain*, based on *natural aversion*. It is not derived from *reactivation* of a *traumatic incident*. See *natural aversion* and compare *secondary pain*.

Primary Traumatic Incident: An incident containing *pain* (emotional and/or physical) where there is actual impact or injury or actual loss that causes the pain. A primary traumatic incident may or may not be the earliest (*root*) incident in the *sequence*. Compare *secondary traumatic incident*.

PRO (Used in *Unstacking*): The quality of being aligned with, allied to, or on the side of the *viewer* in a conflict, either now or from a past viewpoint. If the viewer is a firefighter, the *identity* "a firefighter" might be a PRO identity for them and the *goal* "to fight fires" might be a PRO goal. Compare *CON*.

Problem: An *incongruity* that is of concern or importance to a *person* at a particular time. A *thing* that conflicts with or resists a person's *intention*.

Product: A *thing* that is created as part of an *ideal situation* or that is conducive to its attainment.

Program: A set of *viewing techniques*, presented in the order that is optimum for most *viewers*, intended to address a particular kind of issue encountered in life or in *viewing*. Compare *collection, case plan*.

Proponent: (Used in *Unstacking*) A *PRO identity* in a *stack*. Compare opponent.

PTSD: See *Post-Traumatic Stress Disorder*.

Purpose: An *intention* that continues indefinitely. Compare *goal*.

Purpose of Viewing: The purpose of *viewing* is to relieve *charge*, find *insight*, increase *awareness*, improve ability, and enhance relationships. The intent is to help the *viewer* improve their environment, including their mental environment.

Reaction: An unconsciously arrived at, automatic way of thinking, feeling, or behaving when confronted with a situation. Compare *response*.

Reactivate: To remind a *person*, knowingly or unknowingly, of a *traumatic incident* or *sequence*. To activate or *trigger* a traumatic incident or sequence of incidents. When this occurs, people can re-enact or re-experience parts of the traumatic incident or incidents of which they are reminded, and can often experience uncomfortable or painful feelings.

Reactivated: Of a *traumatic incident* or *sequence*: the state of having been *triggered*, brought back into an active state, impinging on the *person*, by reason of something that has reminded them, consciously or unconsciously, of the traumatic incident or sequence. Once reactivated, it becomes more easily triggered thereafter.

Reactivation: An instance of being reactivated by some *trigger*.

Reality: For an individual *person*, reality is that person's world, what the person believes to exist. Reality, for two or more people, is a "common world", a set of *things* that are shared as a result of *concurrence*.

Realization: An acquisition of new *knowledge* by *understanding*. A common component of an *end point* in *viewing*.

Recall Lists: A collection of extensive lists covering various aspects of life, consisting of mostly pleasant memories; useful for improving memory and for building confidence. Also the *viewing technique* that uses these lists.

Receiving: The action of a *person* taking something in, getting something, inflowing something from their *world*. It is moving something toward the person in the *person-world dimension*.

Reception: See *receptive action*.

Receptive: A directionality along the *polar dimension* toward the *person* from the *world*. Receiving, rather than giving. Pulling in, rather than pushing out.

Receptive Ability: See *understanding*.

Receptive Action: An action of pulling in or receiving already-existing *things* from the world or from another *person*. See *receiving*.

Receptive Technique: A *viewing technique* in which the *viewer* is asked to perform one or more *receptive actions*.

Recovery: A *remedy* used to handle a situation of having gone past an *end point*. In a recovery technique, the *viewer* is returned, as much as possible, to the favorable state they were in at the end point, before it was missed and the viewing activity was continued.

Reduction: The partial or complete elimination of *charge* by a process of *deactivation* or *discharge*.

Referent: The *concept* or *phenomenon* to which a *token* refers.

Reflexive Flow: Causation from self to self.

Relief: Negative pleasure derived from a diminution of *pain* or discomfort. It is one of the major goals a *person* seeks in attempting to organize their *world*. See also *aesthetics*, *deficiency motivation*.

Reliving: The unconscious re-experiencing or re-enactment of one or more *traumatic incidents* that have been *reactivated* but not *discharged*. Reliving can cause *aberrations*, i.e., *delusions*, painful or uncomfortable feelings, or *acting out behavior*. Compare *remembering*, *reviewing*.

Remedy: 1. A brief *viewing technique* used to bring someone swiftly to a better condition, especially in situations where a formal *session* is not practical. 2. A usually brief technique used to handle unforeseen errors or difficulties that may come up during a session.

Remembering: Simply contacting a past event or incident. Compare *reviewing*, *reliving*.

Repeating: A *viewing* pattern used to relieve *charge* in which the *viewer* is asked, repeatedly, to say a phrase aloud. Each time they say it, they view the *concept* expressed in the phrase. Often, the concept has been something they have been saying to themselves sub-vocally and automatically; saying it vocally and consciously takes over the *automaticity* and brings it under their control. As the viewer repeats the phrase, it may change. A better or more accurate way of expressing the concept may come to mind. In this case, the viewer can continue by repeating the new phrase. A phrase may change several times before the viewer is finished with repeating it, or it may not change at all. Repeating can also be used to unstick a *traumatic incident* in *Traumatic Incident Reduction* when a stuck phrase is holding it in place.

Repetition: Repetition allows a *viewing technique*, which if done once would have a very superficial effect, to penetrate into deeper layers of the *viewer's case*. Repetition is also used in training exercises to help someone acquire a *skill*. Repeating something many times can establish a habit pattern that can then be made automatic, or incorporated into one of the *identities* a *person* uses in life (such as that of a pianist). But repetition can also break already established *aberrated* habit patterns (*automatisms*). If you can get someone to do self-determinedly and repeatedly something that was an automatism, the automatism eventually breaks down, temporarily or permanently. See *Unlayering*.

Report Channel: The communication channel along which the *viewer* reports on compliance with *viewing instructions* and the results of carrying out these instructions. Compare *viewing channel*, *instruction channel*.

Repression: Directed unawareness. The act of trying to become unaware of a specific *thing*. Repression is unawareness based on *aversion*, or a flinch from *pain*. It is unconsciousness of a specific *thing* or type of *thing*. and it is brought about by the presence of that *thing* or by the presence of a related (similar) *thing*. Whereas *simple unawareness* is caused by turning toward something else, repression is caused by pointedly turning away from the *thing* of which one is trying to be unconscious.

Resentment: A level on the *Emotional Scale* that lies above Hidden Hostility and below Anger. At this level, one feels angry but does not yet feel capable of doing very much about it. This is the level at which one "holds a grudge". The *condition* in the world that corresponds to Resentment (and to all the emotions from Hidden Hostility through *Ambivalence*) is *Drudgery*.

Resilience Section: That part of the *Curriculum* that addresses *charge* on the subject of change and *upsets*. On completion of this section, the *viewer* will be more resilient—less affected by and more easily recovering from *upsets* and changes.

Resolution Section: That part of the *Curriculum* that addresses *problems*. On completing this section, the *viewer* will be more resolute and will have a better idea of where their problems come from and how to resolve them.

Respect: Allowing someone, without judgment, to be the *identity* that they are being.

Response: A consciously chosen action taken to deal with a *situation*. Compare *reaction*.

Responsibility: Conscious causativeness.

Retraumatization: Happens when someone's *traumas* become *triggered* and are not resolved; i.e., the *person* is effectively put back into the middle of a traumatic experience. This can happen either in life situations or in sessions that are meant to be therapeutic. Though *TIR* has clients review traumatic incidents, *retraumatization* is avoided by the use of *repetition* to reduce all of the *emotional charge* from the incident and also by taking each *viewing action* to an *end point*, where the incident is resolved to the client's satisfaction.

Retrospection: A *viewing* pattern consisting of moving backward in time along lines of similarity; going "earlier similar". Because of the structure of the *traumatic incident network*, retrospection is an especially fruitful pattern to use.; it is employed for instance, in *Basic TIR*, *Disturbance Handling*, and *assessment lists.*

Revenge: A type of *justification* for a *misdeed*. It is the claim that, in acting against a *person*, you are merely paying that person back for what they have done to you: "evening the score". This justification is characteristic of the emotional level of Antagonism.

Reviewing: Going through a past incident, experiencing it in as much detail as possible. This is the heart of the *TIR* technique. Reviewing differs from simple *remembering* as a motion picture differs from a snapshot and it differs from *reliving* in that the *viewer* has conscious control over the process.

Rightness Section: The *viewer*, like anyone else, is of the opinion that what they believe is right. Otherwise, they wouldn't believe it. But they can be righter. Wrongnesses can be caused by *misconceptions*, false information, or *fixed ideas*. This section addresses all three. On completing this section, one will *actually* be righter, and one will have less of a compulsion to *assert* one's rightness.

Root: The *traumatic incident* that is earliest in a *sequence* and on which the entire sequence relies for its existence. It contains natural aversion (*primary pain*). It does not merely contain aversion based on a reminder of an earlier incident (*secondary pain*). Compare *sequent*.

Rules of Consultation: Rules followed by an *AMP* practitioner in the role of a *consultant*, including limited *evaluation* and advice in the service of the client's needs. The consultant does not do anything for clients that they can do for themselves.

Rules of Facilitation: Strict rules a *facilitator* follows to ensure that *facilitation* occurs in a safe space.

Schema Program A series of specific tasks done to create a model for understanding life, and a plan or set of plans for reaching *goals* and fulfilling *purposes*. A schema program may entail a systematic arrangement and analysis of a client's entire life, or it may be limited to being a systematic arrangement and analysis of a particular *domain* or of a specific *activity* in which the client is or wants to be *engaged*.

Schema Work: See *Life Planning.*

Schema Workshop: See *Life Coaching Schema Workshop.*

Secondary Gain: The "usefulness" of *aberration*, apart from its function in facilitating *repression*. For instance, a *person* may cultivate or exaggerate an upset or psychosomatic condition in order to get help, attention, or money from others.

Secondary Pain: *Pain* derived from reactivation of an earlier *traumatic incident* on the *sequence*. Compare *primary pain*.

Secondary Traumatic Incident: An incident in which the *pain* is derived from *reactivation* of an earlier incident (or incidents). A secondary traumatic incident cannot be the first (*root*) incident of a *sequence*. Compare *primary traumatic incident*.

Second Consideration: A *consideration* made that is *incongruent* with a *first consideration* that is already in place and not unmade. Making a second consideration is a means of *repression*. It consists of adding a layer of *delusion* on top of one's first consideration about something. There can also be a third consideration, a fourth consideration, etc.

Second Domain: See *Intimates*.

Selecting: A powerful *viewing method* used in just one *viewing technique*: Selection, that addresses a charged subject that is unclear in some fundamental way. The *viewer* is asked a specific sort of question. The viewer gives answers, and the *facilitator* writes them down as a list. Together the viewer and facilitator discover the one answer to that question that is correct for that viewer at that time. Finding the correct answer allows the viewer to clarify the matter, as a pattern of realignment takes place in the viewer's mental world like a cascade of different waterfalls into a single channel that is the right answer for the viewer at that time. The same question may generate another right answer at another time.

Self-Determinism: The consideration that one is responsible for one's own actions and interests but not for others'. A self-determined *person* plays *zero-sum games*. Compare *other-determinism, multi-determinism*.

Sequence: A group of one or more related or associated *traumatic incidents*, connected by one or more types of *triggers* or *themes* in which later traumatic incidents contain elements that trigger earlier ones.

Sequent: A *traumatic incident* that is not the *root* for a particular *sequence* but is based on *reactivation* of a root or another sequent. Besides a *trigger* of an earlier traumatic incident in the sequence, it may also contain *primary pain*, as well as one or more other elements that fit a different sequence.

Sequential Unlayering: An *unlayering* technique, such as *Unblocking*, that consists of going down a set of questions, using repetition to carry each question with available *charge* on it to an *end point* or *flat point* as one goes along. The technique as a whole is carried to an end point where the *viewer* has a significant shift on the topic being addressed and/or the viewer has no more available charge on the area being addressed.

Session: In the context of Applied Metapsychology, including *Traumatic Incident Reduction*, a session is a period of time, flexible in length, that is bound by the *Rules of Facilitation* or the *Rules of Consultation*, structured according to the *Communication Exercises* and the protocols of the specific techniques employed.

Session Agenda: A written list of the actions the *facilitator* plans to take in the next *viewing session*.

Shedding: The relinquishing of an *identity* in favor of a more general identity through the disincorporation of previously incorporated elements. Compare *assumption (of an identity)*.

Sidetrack: An unnecessary deviation from a *viewing technique* or *program*. More generally a , failure to follow through and complete an *activity cycle*. In *viewing*, a sidetrack tries to handle something that either requires no handling or would be handled adequately by merely continuing the current technique. Compare d*etour*.

Significance: The *conceptual* and *factual* content of an experience, such as the ideas encountered in study, as opposed to the *phenomenal* content, such as mental pictures or physical *objects*. Something that cannot be the *object* of *action, communication*, or *perception*. It is an idea or relationship, not a *thing* or *person* you can relate to directly. Motherhood, intelligence, and cleanliness are significances, not objects. Compare *mass*, f*orce*.

Simple Retrospection: The action of describing an *incident* or *item*, then tracing it back to earlier similar incidents or items, giving a simple description of each. Unlike *TIR*, it does not involve re-experiencing or *reliving* past incidents or contacting the same incident repetitively, nor does it involve a series of steps. It simply involves description, followed by finding an earlier similar incident or *item*, until an *end point* occurs.

Simple Unawareness: A normal and *unaberrated unawareness*; a consequence of the fact that a *person* does not have an unlimited ability or desire to be *aware* of things. Examples include the unawareness we have of things we take for granted or that are part of our skill set, forgetfulness caused by the passage of time, unawareness of things that are irrelevant to a particular *purpose* or *identity*, and unawareness of things that were never *known*. Compare *repression*.

Simple Unlayering: A *viewing method* consisting of a single *viewing instruction*, repeated as many times as necessary, to an *end point*.

Simplicity: The first major sub-category of *order*. As per *Occam's Razor*, people will, all else being equal, opt for simplicity in their data. This means that they will want to have a world with as few separate parts as possible. They will want the elements of their experience to be as non-complex as possible. A world which is terribly complex is hard to keep track of. A *person* will, for instance, prefer a simple tax form to a complex one, and a simple explanation to a complex one.

Situation: A *thing* described as a form or as a relation amongst other *things,* existing at a particular point in time. Compare *object, event*. See also *current situation, ideal situation*.

Situational Aversions: Situational aversions can be understood from an examination of the basic ways in which people seem to organize their experience. These *aversions* exist regardless of one's bodily state. One seeks to maximize one's *power* to handle one's world and the degree of *communion* one has with other people. One has an aversion to circumstances or *situations* that would prevent one from doing so.

Situational Pain: *Primary pain* that is non-physical but derived from the presence of a situation (such as a *misdeed*, a *withhold*, a *problem*, disorder, lack of control, tedium, etc.) for which people have a natural aversion because it decreases their *power* or *communion*.

Skill: An *ability* of which a *person* has a *simple (not directed) unawareness*, because the ability has been incorporated as part of an *identity* the person has assumed. A learned *automaticity*. Compare *automatism*.

Social Identity: The way in which one chooses to appear to others. Ideally one's social identity is congruent with one's actual *identity*. Otherwise one lacks *integrity* and is being a *phony*.

Space: A set of three *dimensions* that separate *things* from each other by position, such as right/left, up/down, in/out. Compare *time*.

Stability: A major sub-category of *order*. One of the main features that exists for a *person* in an optimal world. A very unstable world is a disorderly one that is hard to live in.

Stack (used in *Unstacking*): A series of *dichotomies*, thought to lie at the core of the *traumatic incident network*, that share a common key concept. This concept, like the *theme* in a *sequence* of traumatic incidents, is the common denominator that ties together all the dichotomies in a given stack by establishing a common "playing field" for all those dichotomies.

State of Affairs: See *situation*.

Stress: The condition of being confronted with something that seems overwhelming or that one thinks one may be incapable of *confronting* or *handling*. It is a relationship between a *person* and the environment that borders on being traumatic. Compare *traumatic incident*, *challenge*.

Stressor: A *thing* or *person* one regards as causing stress.

Student Facilitator: The student in a training exercise who is working to improve their skill in some specific facet of *facilitation*; the student who takes the role of *facilitator* in an exercise.

Subjective: On or toward the *mind* side of the *person-world polarity*.

Subjective Technique: A *viewing technique* whose *item* or items are located in the past or in the *mind*. *Receptive* subjective techniques are designed to increase one's degree of insight into, and *understanding* of, one's past and one's mind. These techniques improve one's ability to *perceive, interpret*, and *understand* parts of their subjective *world*. *Creative* subjective techniques exercise the ability to *conceive* ideas and make mental pictures. Often, such techniques (as with many *creative techniques*) are useful in gaining control of unwanted automatic actions or conditions, such as bad habits.

Subjectivity: The quality of an object being on the *person* side of the *person-world polarity* (the *mind*). See *objectivity, polar dimension*.

Success: The fulfillment of an *intention* or (equivalently) the completion of an *activity cycle*.

Table of Attitudes: A chart showing how different categories of experience, such as *having, control , success*, etc., align with the *Emotional Scale* and with each other.

Taking Over: Taking *control* and *responsibility* for an *automatism* and thus causing it to cease to be automatic. By taking over an automatic action, a *person* regains causativeness over it. By taking responsibility for doing something, one acquires the ability to stop doing it.

Target: A step in an *action plan*.

Task: An *activity* one knowingly engages in.

Technical Directing (or Technical Direction): The activity of a technical director writing *case plans*, reviewing, consulting about and improving individualized case plans written by *facilitators* for use with *viewers* and making sure they are *facilitating* correctly.

Technical Director (TD): The person who plans and oversees *facilitation* and makes sure that *facilitators* are doing their jobs well. The TD makes sure that *viewers* and facilitators get help and support promptly if any difficulties arise. The TD helps correct and teach the facilitator as needed. "Supervisor" could be used as a synonym here. Though facilitators often act as their own technical directors, it is useful to be clear on the concepts of the two roles.

Technique: A set of *viewing instructions* designed to address a certain type of charged *case* material (such as *traumatic incidents*, *upsets*, *charge* on a specific *person*, etc.) and meant to be continued to an *end point*.

Thematic Item: See **Theme**.

Thematic TIR (TTIR): The form of *TIR* that deals with *sequences* of *traumatic incidents*, all of which have a certain *theme* in common, and traces them back to the first trauma or *root* incident of that sequence. Compare *Basic TIR*.

Theme: An unwanted feeling, emotion, sensation, attitude or *pain* (*FESAP*) that is common to the different *traumatic incidents* in a *sequence*, serving to link them together. Themes are not patterns of behavior in a *person*'s life, such as a tendency to enter into abusive relationships. Themes appear automatically in a person's experience, outside of the person's *control*.

Thing: An *object*, *event*, or *situation* that is part of a *person*'s world, i.e., that exists for a person at a certain moment. The word is italicized to differentiate it from normal usage. Compare *person*.

Time: A *dimension* that separates *things* from each other according to tense. In time, as in space, people find themselves in the present at the origin, and past and future are in opposite directions.

TIR: *Traumatic Incident Reduction.*

TIR for Children: A form of simplified TIR that works well with children.

Token: A *phenomenon* that indicates or refers to something else. A phenomenon that has meaning. The word "red" (spoken or written) is a token that refers to a certain wavelength of light or a certain type of visual phenomenon; dark clouds can be a token of rain.

Trainer: An instructor in an *Applied Metapsychology* workshop. Compare *tutor,*

Transcendent Experience: An experience that gives a *person* a clear impression of self as a spiritual being, not co-extensive with the body, because the experience appears to transcend the limits of a purely physical model of the universe. These events might include: the appearance of past lives, contact with other beings close to the *viewer* that are not inhabiting bodies, *out-of-body experiences*, ESP experiences, and religiously transcendent experiences.

Trauma: See traumatic incident.

Traumatic Incident: An incident that is wholly or partially *repressed* and that contains *charge* and a greater or lesser degree of *pain*—felt, created, or received. A *receptive action* that is incomplete and thus undischarged because of repression.

Traumatic Incident Network (Net): The network composed of all of the *person's* traumatic incidents, with their various interconnections.

Traumatic Incident Reduction (TIR): A *viewing technique* that is akin to certain early psychoanalytical techniques. It involves tracing back *sequences* of traumatic incidents to their *roots* while completing the incomplete *receptive cycles* that have accumulated in the sequences and finishing with an *end point. Thematic TIR* starts with an incident containing a particular theme and proceeds back to earlier incidents with the same theme, while the *Basic TIR* technique starts with a known incident and may or may not involve going back to earlier similar incidents.

Traumatic Incident Reduction for Children Workshop (TIRC): A usually two-day training (*TIR workshop* is the prerequisite) teaching specialized approaches for working with children on both traumatic incidents and other issues using TIR and related techniques.

Traumatic Incident Reduction – Expanded Applications Workshop (TIR-EA): A four day second level workshop designed to follow the *TIR Workshop* and having it as a prerequisite. It provides further applications of TIR in new techniques, an additional array of techniques for addressing life situations. It also introduces the *Addictions Program*, and teaches the *chart method of case planning*. See also *Life Stress Reduction Workshop. (LSRW)*.

Traumatic Incident Reduction Workshop: A four or five day training workshop that teaches the basic skills of *Applied Metapsychology*, and well as the major techniques of TIR and *Unblocking*. A first level training.

Trigger (noun): A *thing* that reminds a *person*, knowingly or unknowingly, of a *traumatic incident*, a *sequence*, or another *charged* subject.

Trigger (verb): To cause someone to experience a *disturbance*; to *reactivate* one or more of that *person*'s *traumatic incidents*.

Truth: The *factuality* of a *concept*, its condition of being *assented* to or believed with certainty by a *person*. In a *person-centered context*, there is no "absolute truth".

Turning Point: The point in *viewing* at which one becomes aware that one is separate from one's *case* even when one is manifesting or feeling the effects of it. The state of being more causative over one's *case* than one is the effect of it, of not having to act on the dictates of one's case.

Tutor: In training, the student who is coaching their partner in a training exercise for the purpose of improving the skill of the partner; differentiated from the *trainer*, who is the person conducting the course or workshop. A tutor often takes the role of *viewer* in training exercises.

Unawareness: Lack of *awareness*. There are two kinds of unawareness: *simple unawareness* and directed unawareness (*repression*).

Unblocking: A technique in which a number of mental blocks on a certain issue are addressed repetitively until *charge* has been addressed and *awareness* increased on that subject.

Unburdened: Free of current *reactivation* and *disturbances*.

Unburdening: An action taken to *deactivate* or *discharge* material that is *reactivated* in life or in a *session*. The *end point* of unburdening is a *viewer* who is free of *disturbances* and immediately troubling life issues and ready to move on to *Ability Enhancement*. See also *disturbance handling*.

Underlying Truth: A *concept* that is closer to a *first consideration* than the relative falsehood or falsehoods that it underlies. See *delusion, second consideration*.

Understanding (verb): The *creation* of a new *fact* from one or more *data*. A *concept* arrived at by *interpretation* of a datum or data, being a concept, is a candidate fact. What makes it an actual fact is an act of *assent*. The combination of interpreting and *acceptance* is called "understanding". When one understands one or more data, one arrives at a new fact, a *conclusion*.

Understanding (noun): *Receptive ability*, the ability to exercise receptive abilities on a *thing* or on the world. Understanding is that quality in the *person* that corresponds to *heuristics* or learning potential in the person's world. Compare *control, comprehension*.

Unfinished Business: A technique for addressing a problematic relationship, where the person in question is unavailable, through death, absence, or estrangement,

Unintelligibility: That quality of a *datum* by virtue of which it resists *understanding*.

Unlayering: A type of *viewing technique* which consists of a *repetition* of a certain *viewing action* to remove *charge* and reach an *end point*.

Unstacking: A technique for locating and discharging sets of conflicting *goals* and *identities*, called *stacks*.

Unwanted Feeling: A feeling, emotion, sensation, attitude, or *pain* that is unwanted, caused by unresolved *charge*.

Upset: A sudden or unexpected lowering of *communion* or *power*.

Verification: The action of determining the correctness or acceptability of an *interpretation* or *concept*, following certain rules for maximizing *power* and *communion*. These rules are the means by which the *person* moves, in the integration phase of the *learning cycle*, from having a mere concept as an interpretation of the available *data*, to an *acceptance* of that concept as *factual*.

Versatility: The ability to *assume* or *shed identities*.

Very Positive Indicators (VPIs): *Indicators* that a *viewer* is most likely to display at an *end point*, or at other points where one is being successful, such as laughing, having *realizations*, and appearing bright and *extroverted*. Very positive indicators accompany any full end point.

Viewer: The one in a *viewing session* whose role is to examine their world and arrive at *insights* concerning it. *Viewing* is done by the viewer, not by the *facilitator*. Viewers should not be concerned with the mechanics of the session or the *session agenda*. They should only be concerned with viewing.

Viewing: An activity in which a *person* systematically examines their world in such a way as to gain *insight* and *ability* by undoing *repression*; a systematic, one-on-one method for exploring and bringing order and clarity to one's own *mind*. Viewing is purely a form of *integrative learning*.

Viewing Channel: In a *session*, the channel along which the *viewer* contacts the material they are *viewing*. Compare *instruction channel*, *report channel*.

Viewing Instruction: A part of a *viewing technique* consisting of an instruction given to a *viewer* by a *facilitator*. The facilitator *acknowledges* the *viewer's* execution of the instruction.

Viewing Question: A *viewing instruction* consisting of a question asked of a *viewer* by a *facilitator*. Compliance with the instruction consists of answering the question. The facilitator *acknowledges* the viewer's answer.

Viewing Session: A *session* in which *viewing* occurs. Compare *consultation session*.

Viewing Technique: A technique used in *viewing* to address *charge*. It is carried to an *end point*.

Volition: The *intention* to *create*. Compare *attention*.

Willingness: The absence of *counter-intention*.

Wish: A *desire* for something to whose absence the *person* does *not* have an *aversion*. Compare *need*.

Withhold: Something that a *person knows* but does not reveal to others when an occasion arises to do so.

Work: An *activity engaged* in at an emotional level of Complacency or below. The only difference between *work* and *play* is the emotional level at which it is done.

World: That which the *person perceives*, that which they *know* or *understand*, that upon which they *act*, and that which they *create*, by means of and from the viewpoint of an *identity*; the totality of what exists for them at a certain moment, including their *mind*, other people, and what they perceive or know of the physical universe.

Worry: A *problem* that is currently occupying the *person's attention* and will continue to do so until it is resolved.

Wrong Indication: (WI) An *evaluative* and usually *invalidative statement* that violates the recipient's self-concept and perception of truth.

Wrong Indication Handling: 1. Addressing and resolving a *wrong indication* as a *remedy*, when one pops up in the course of a *session*. 2. Systematically searching out and resolving large numbers of wrong indications as a major *case* action, a very powerful *technique*.

Zero-Sum Game: A game in which the more there is for one player, the less there is for the others. If one wins a zero-sum game, the others lose. *Self-determined* individuals play zero-sum games. Compare *non-zero-sum game* and *multi-determinism*.

Commonly Used Abbreviations in Applied Metapsychology

AA: *Automatic attention*

ACEs: *Adverse Childhood Experiences*

AEW: *Ability Enhancement Workshop*

AMI: *Applied Metapsychology International*

AMP: *Applied metapsychology*

BTIR: *Basic TIR*

CEs: *Communication exercises*

Cycle: *Activity cycle*

F1, F2, F3, F4: Flows 1, 2, 3, 4—*Inflow, Outflow, Crossflow,* and *Reflexive Flow.*

EP: *End point*

EI: Either "earlier, similar incident" in *Basic TIR* or "Earlier incident containing _____ [*theme/FESAP*]" in *Thematic TIR*

EOS: End of session

ES: *Earlier starting point*

E/Sim: *Earlier, similar*

FESAPs   *Feelings, emotions, sensations, attitudes and pains*

FP: *Flat point*

FTIR: *Future TIR*

GTI:	*Get the Idea*
L/H:	"Is this incident getting lighter or heavier?"
LSL:	*Life Stress List*
LSR:	*Life Stress Reduction*
LSRW:	*Life Stress Reduction Workshop*
LTT:	*Long-term Trauma Handling*
MO:	*Modus operandi*
Net:	*Traumatic incident network*
NIs:	*Negative indicators*
OBE:	*Out-of-body experience*
PIs:	*Positive indicators*
PTIR:	*Pleasant TIR*
PTSD:	*Post-traumatic stress disorder*
SOS:	Start of session
TD:	*Technical director.*
TIR:	*Traumatic incident reduction*
TIRC:	*Traumatic Incident Reduction for Children Workshop*
TIR–EA:	*TIR – Expanded Applications Workshop*
TIRW:	*Traumatic Incident Reduction Workshop*
TTIR:	*Thematic TIR*
VPIs:	*Very positive indicators*
W/H:	*Withhold*
WI:	*Wrong indication* or *Wrong Indication Handling*

About Applied Metapsychology International

Applied Metapsychology International (AMI) (first called the Institute for Research in Metapsychology), was founded by Frank A. Gerbode, MD in 1984 for the purpose of developing, researching, and disseminating the subject of Applied Metapsychology. AMI is a U.S. 501(c)3 US non-profit corporation.

The Board of Directors oversees the overall direction and plans of the organization. Committees perform many of the vital functions of the organization, such Development & Editing, running the Certification program, co-coordinating Research, and so on.

AMI holds the copyrights of the materials and maintains a certification program that sets standards of service. The certification process offers students who have successfully completed facilitator (practitioner) training the opportunity to improve and develop their capabilities and be recognized as competent.

After an in-depth apprenticeship, new trainers may be certified to deliver the training workshops, and to supervise the work of other facilitators.

Since its conception, AMI has continued to support, encourage, and oversee research in TIR and related techniques around the world.

Person-Centered Techniques Put You Back in Control of Your Destiny

Metapsychology is the science of human nature and experience as viewed by you-- the one who experiences--from the inside out, not by an outside "expert" trying to look in. The methods of "Applied Metapsychology" recognize you as the authority at the center of your world of experience, and provide tools to enable you to improve personal relationships, increase personal power, and fashion your world into the loving, fascinating, and fulfilling place you always wanted it to be. Readers of this book will learn...

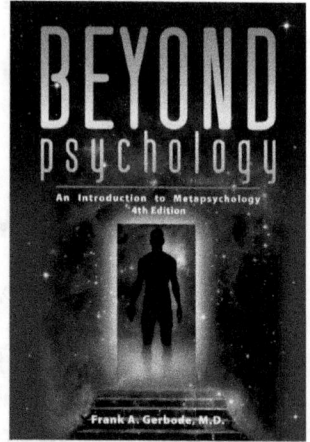

- The principles and methodology of Applied Metapsychology, a truly effective method for understanding yourself, your own mind, and your world of experience

- The principles of Traumatic Incident Reduction (TIR), a technique for resolving the traumatic incidents that build upon each other to produce a network of distress that can lead to Post Traumatic Stress Disorder (PTSD).

- Specific other techniques to help you address the issues which concern you most--relationships, job satisfaction, and unwanted emotions such as grief and anger.

- A systematic method of case-planning for designing coherent and effective strategies for achieving these ends in a relatively short period of time.

"Beyond Psychology deserves to be widely known, studied and applied. A new synthesis is now possible."
-- Lewis H. Gann, Ph.D., Senior Fellow, Hoover Institution, Stanford University

For more information please visit **www.TIRBook.com**

From Applied Metapsychology International Press

www.ingramcontent.com/pod-product-compliance
Lightning Source LLC
LaVergne TN
LVHW021135080426
835509LV00010B/1363

Applied Metapsychology Dictionary

The term "metapsychology" (small m) means, briefly: The science that unifies mental and physical experience. Its purpose is to discover the rules that apply to both. It is a study of the person, their abilities and experience, as seen from their own point of view. Applied Metapsychology (AMP) is the subject that puts the principles of metapsychology to work for the purpose of relieving traumatic stress, promoting personal growth and development, and empowering people to improve the quality of their lives.

This dictionary includes most of the terms used in Applied Metapsychology. Working out a proper and consistent vocabulary for metapsychology has been a continual compromise between what sounds graceful in ordinary English and what conveys a precise meaning. Many of our terms also occur in normal speech in a sense similar to, but usually not exactly the same as, that given here, just as physics uses terms like "mass", "density", and "energy" in a specialized and more precise way. Natural language is preferred instead of inventing new terms, because their meaning is similar enough to normal usage to give the reader an intuitive idea of what is meant, while the metapsychological definition provides the needed precision for the subject.

An appendix of this dictionary contains some commonly used abbreviations and acronyms in the subject of Applied Metapsychology.

Learn more at www.TIRBook.com

US$14.95

ISBN 978-1-61599-474-8

51495

9 781615 994748

AMI
Press